A GIFT FOR

Nicole Shindler
....

"Love"
FROM

Grandma & Grandpa
....

Christmas 2004

D1165284

the Christmas Troll

ILLUSTRATED BY WILL TERRY

Eugene H. Peterson

NAVPRESS®

BRINGING TRUTH TO LIFE

NavPress
P.O. Box 35001
Colorado Springs, Colorado 80935

www.navpress.com

NAVPRESS, BRINGING TRUTH TO LIFE, and the NAVPRESS logo are registered trademarks of NavPress. Absence of ® in connection with marks of NavPress or other parties does not indicate an absence of registration of those marks.

This story was originally published in *Mars Hill Review,* a two-hundred-page journal of essays, studies, and reminders of God. For more information, please contact 1-800-990-MARS or visit www.marshillreview.com.

ISBN 1-57683-681-9

Design by The DesignWorks Group, www.thedesignworksgroup.com
Illustration by Will Terry
Creative Team: Arvid Wallen, Don Simpson, Cara Iverson

Printed in China

1 2 3 4 5 6 7 8 9 10 / 08 07 06 05 04

FOR A FREE CATALOG OF
NAVPRESS BOOKS & BIBLE STUDIES,
CALL 1-800-366-7788 (USA)
OR 1-416-499-4615 (CANADA)

FOR SADIE LYNN

*who arrived too late to meet
the Christmas troll*

It was Christmas Eve and Andrew was angry—very angry. He hunched his shoulders and scowled the way angry people do in the TV cartoons. He decided to run away from home. He grabbed the hand of his little sister. "C'mon, Lindsay," he said, and they headed for the woods.

The woods were dark and frightening, and Andrew was forbidden to go there alone. But he had Lindsay with him, so he wasn't actually alone. Lindsay had saucer eyes and thought everything he did was wonderful. She didn't mind that Andrew was angry, because she knew they were on another adventure. Andrew was nearly grown up—he was six years old—and was always taking her on adventures.

The forest started at the end of their street. There was just enough light from Andrew's lantern to show them where the trail entered the trees. Sometimes on Saturday afternoon their parents would take them on tramps through the woods. Andrew and Lindsay would run ahead and hide behind fallen logs or big rocks and then jump out and scare their parents. Their father scared best. He would throw up his arms and yell and try to climb a tree. Then he would grab them and toss them up in the air and they would all laugh together. But they had never been here in the dark before. The huge trees were taller and thicker than they'd ever seen them.

Andrew couldn't tell whether the dark shadows were fallen trees and boulders or crouching bears and hulking trolls.

He began to get scared, but then he felt Lindsay's hand in his and became brave again, at least brave enough to go on a little farther. And then he remembered how angry he was and that he was running away from home, and that made him even braver.

Besides, he wasn't sure there really were trolls in the woods. It was Jonathan who had told him about trolls, but Jonathan lied a lot. Jonathan lived next door and was a bully. He was always making up stories to try to scare Andrew.

No, he wasn't at all sure about trolls. Jonathan said that trolls were ugly and mean. They had big bellies and bottoms balanced over stubby legs. Toes grew out of both ends of their feet, six in front and six in back, so if you saw their tracks in the mud or snow, you couldn't tell whether they were coming or going.

And their faces were put together any which way.

A troll might have a nose on each side of its head and an ear in the middle of its face, or eyes in its chin and a mouth grinning horribly out of the back of its head. But mostly, Andrew didn't believe Jonathan.

And anyway, right now he was too angry to worry over trolls.

All Andrew had wanted to do was open one Christmas present from under the tree, and his mother wouldn't let him. By now Jonathan had opened nearly all his presents. Jonathan had started begging weeks ago, and his parents always gave in. All Andrew had wanted was to open one present on Christmas Eve—just one. He knew he couldn't wait until morning to see what he'd get. Not only had his mother refused, but when he wouldn't quit asking, she had sent him from the supper table before he could finish his dessert—his favorite Christmas dessert of baked apple with cinnamon and honey on it. He'd then tried begging his father, "Please, just one present?

I can't wait to see what I'm getting!"

But he got no further with his father. "Gifts are for giving and receiving," his father had said, "not for grabbing and getting. Waiting until morning will be good for you."

Christmas was ruined. He hated Christmas. He was glad to be running away. It felt good to leave. When his mother and father found out that he had run away, they would be sorry.

Andrew and Lindsay were deep in the woods now. The trees were bigger than ever, the bushes and boulders blacker than ever. Andrew wondered how much farther they had to go to run away, really run away. He hoped not too much farther. He looked down at Lindsay, her hand holding tightly to his. "Do you think we ought to rest, Lindsay? Let's find a log to sit on and take a rest." He wished he had thought to bring some food—a few cookies or nuts or an apple. His mother always remembered to bring food when they tramped through the woods.

He saw a log just the right size for sitting, and they sat down on it. As they sank into the soft, cushioning moss of the log, Andrew thought it was the softest log he had ever sat on and began to feel safe and protected by the softness. Just then there was a long, low rumble like far-off thunder, except the sound was under them. In a few moments the thunder beneath them became a stuttering, gravelly voice:

"Who's s-s-s-sitting on my b-b-b-belly?"

Andrew had never been so frightened. He was sitting on a troll! He ran for his life. He forgot all about Lindsay and ran straight off the trail into the darkness. He tripped on a root, hit his head on a tree, and fell crumpled into a clump of ferns. He wanted to cry but was afraid to make any noise. He hoped the ferns would hide him from the troll. Suddenly he remembered Lindsay, left behind on the huge, mossy belly of the troll. What was happening to her?

Now he was twice scared—scared for Lindsay as well as himself. Would the troll by now have put Lindsay in a cage, cut off all her hair, and put a ring in her nose?

That's what Jonathan said trolls did to lost children—kept them as pets the way we have dogs and cats. But Andrew was too scared to go back.

After what seemed like a long, long time, Andrew heard her voice, faint and sweet, calling him through the darkness: "Drew... Drew... it's okay.

The troll is ugly—but nice."

Slowly and gradually the scaring left him. He crawled out of the ferns and followed her voice. This time he didn't trip over any roots or bang into any trees. Soon he was back on the trail and saw Lindsay sitting on the troll's belly, except now the troll was not a stretched-out log but a stump—a thick, round stump of a troll bouncing Lindsay on his big jello-soft belly and laughing in a gentle, gravelly chuckle. Before he knew it, he was there, too, laughing and bouncing with Lindsay on the belly of the troll.

He was ugly all right, that troll, but not in the way Jonathan had said. All the parts of his face were in the right places—it's just that they were all the wrong size and seemed to have been put on just a little crooked. His nose came slantwise down his face, starting its descent at the edge of his left eye and ending with a flourishing swoop at the right corner of his mouth and with nose hairs sticking out of his nostrils. But really what you saw when you looked at him was hair, for his head was thick with hair—spiky, carrot-colored hair.

Andrew's favorite new word these days was "ridiculous." He wasn't quite sure what it meant, but he loved saying it, loved the sound of it, and said it a lot: "Ree-dick-you-luss, ree-dick-you-luss." All at once, he knew exactly what it meant: It meant this troll, unexpected and funny. It meant something that took you from being scared to having fun in about two seconds. And so Andrew shouted to the troll, "This is ridiculous! *You're* ridiculous!" The troll looked puzzled and then worried. Lindsay, who had heard Andrew say the word a lot but never knew what it meant until then, said, "It's okay, Mr. Troll. It means you're ugly but nice." The troll tried out the new word in his growling, stuttery rumble of a voice—

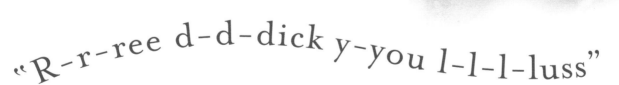

"R-r-ree d-d-dick y-you l-l-l-luss"

—and soon they were all saying it together.

They bounced some more on the belly of the troll, laughed and bounced, chanting, "Ree-dick-you-luss, ree-dick-you-luss."

When the troll laughed, his face got all crinkly like a wadded-up newspaper, the grin on his crooked old face disappearing into his chin.

Suddenly Andrew stopped bouncing and then jumped down from the troll's belly. Lindsay kept on bouncing. Andrew had just remembered that he was supposed to be angry and that he was running away from home and that Christmas was ruined because his mother hadn't let him open even one gift early. But what was this new feeling? He felt like he had hoped to feel on Christmas Eve by opening that gift under the tree: surprised and wonderful. He had just met his first troll and he was feeling fantastic! He wasn't scared and he was having fun and Lindsay was safe.

Usually Lindsay just imitated Andrew, but this time she said, "If you come home with us, I'll get my mother to sing you songs of Jesus. She says that Jesus is God's very best gift. If you heard her sing, you'd know it—she sings like an angel. She'll sing songs about you, too, and then Jonathan will know that you are a gift,

because the best gifts are to sing about and celebrate."

For all their tugging and pleading, the troll wouldn't come with them. Trolls are shy and quiet. They don't mind being ridiculous, and they love being discovered as gifts, but they don't like being treated as someone's toy to be set aside when not being used. So Andrew and Lindsay finally gave up pulling on the troll to come home with them. They both said, "Good-bye, Christmas Troll." Then they left for home.

When they walked through the front door, their parents were still in the kitchen, cleaning up after supper. They hadn't even noticed that Andrew and Lindsay had been gone!

Later in the evening, their mother sang songs about Jesus being born. Their father told them again that the best gifts weren't the wrapped up ones under the tree and so

it's wise to live life expectantly, alert to the surprises of God.

Andrew and Lindsay looked at each other and knew exactly what he was talking about. Had they ever been surprised!

After they had been tucked into bed and blessed by their father, Lindsay lay awake for a long time in the dark, thinking about their adventure with the Christmas troll. She thought about how even though the troll wouldn't come home with them, she took with her the sense of his gentleness and laughter. *Ridiculous!* she thought. Then she remembered that tomorrow was Christmas Day. She whispered,

"Drew, do you think Jesus was ugly but nice?"

But Andrew was fast asleep, dreaming about Jesus in a manger—surprised but pleased in his dream that Jesus had a halo of spiky, carrot-colored hair.

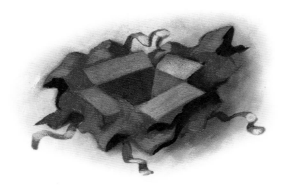